Mollie MAKES

WEDDINGS

♡making ♡thrifting ♡collecting ♡crafting

CONTENTS

HANDMADE
INVITES

BOUQUETS
AND FLOWERS

CRAFTED BLISS

It's the biggest day of your life, and the perfect opportunity to design a party that reflects the two of you! As well as ensuring you get the look you're after, making your nuptials handmade is a great excuse to invite friends and family along before the shindig for some fun craft-alongs. Put loved ones to work on Kirsty Neale's chalkboard feather napkin rings for your place settings or her diamond and tassel garland – a pretty backdrop to summer garden weddings or indoor affairs alike.

We have brought together 20 projects for this compendium of big day ideas from all our favourite *Mollie Makes* designer-makers. Combining crochet, paper, fabric, embellishments, felt, clay and cross stitch, there's a huge range of techniques here to try your hand at; from Ilaria Chiaratti's glass-painted flower displays to Gretel Parker's gorgeous needle felted polar bear cake toppers.

With clear instructions and projects for beginners and experienced crafters, we're sure you'll find something to inspire the most special of occasions. Enjoy!

Lots of love and many congrats from the *Mollie Makes* team,

Lara

Lara Watson
Editor, *Mollie Makes*

STITCHED PAPER
SAVE THE DAY GARLAND

ONCE THE WEDDING DATE HAS BEEN SET, YOU'LL BE KEEN TO LET FRIENDS AND FAMILY KNOW
SO THAT THEY CAN BE SURE TO SAVE THE DAY. THIS QUICK-TO-MAKE GARLAND CAN BE HUNG
TO REMIND YOUR GUESTS OF THE FORTHCOMING EVENT LONG BEFORE THE FORMAL INVITES
ARE SENT OUT. IT CONCERTINA-FOLDS INTO ENVELOPE SLEEVES FOR EASE OF POSTING.

HOW TO MAKE... SAVE THE DAY GARLAND

MATERIALS

THIN CARD IN COLOURS OF YOUR CHOOSING FOR THE ENVELOPE SLEEVES

SELECTION OF PATTERNED PAPERS FOR THE DATE PENNANTS

TRACING PAPER

NARROW RIBBON

NUMBER AND LETTER STAMPS

INK PAD

CUTTING MAT, CRAFT KNIFE AND METAL RULER

SEWING MACHINE

TIP

To create a vintage-style garland, recycle scraps of wrapping paper, postcards, letters and photographs, and look out for wood-block stamps at flea markets.

01 For the envelope sleeves, cut out two rectangles of thin card, one measuring approx 23 x 18cm (9 x 7in) and the other measuring approx 20 x 15cm (8 x 6in). Fold each in half widthways.

02 For the date pennant backgrounds, cut out rectangles from your patterned paper selection, each measuring approx 8 x 11.5cm (3⅛ x 4½in) – one for each number of the date, plus two to use as dividers between the date elements.

03 Cut out rectangles of tracing paper to the exact same size as the patterned paper rectangles. Print each number of the date onto the tracing paper rectangles, and print a decorative motif, such as a small starburst or a heart, for the date dividers. A selection of different typefaces has been used to print the date on our garland, but this is not essential. Pair each of the tracing paper overlays with a patterned paper background to complete the date pennants.

04 Now attach the date pennants to the ribbon. To make sure you cut the ribbon to the right length, lay the date pennants along the ribbon, positioning them with a 1.5cm (⅝in) space in between and extending twice the width of the envelope sleeve plus 4cm (1½in) at each side. Check you have the date in the correct order, then machine stitch the date pennants to the ribbon length.

CLARE YOUNGS

Designer-maker Clare was given a craft book with a pile of paper and fabric at the age of eight and she hasn't stopped making since! Having trained as a graphic designer, she worked in packaging and illustration until turning to craft full time. Clare has written several craft books – to find out more visit www.clareyoungs.co.uk

05 At the left-hand side of the garland, place 4cm (1½in) of the ribbon inside the top edge of the larger of the card envelope sleeves, aligning the top of the ribbon to the edge of the card. Machine stitch close to the top edge of the folded card to secure the ribbon in place. Repeat to attach the ribbon to the smaller of the card envelope sleeves on the right-hand side of the garland (see photo). Machine stitch both envelope sleeves along the bottom edge.

06 Using a small coin as a guide, draw a semicircle halfway down the open-ended edge of the larger envelope sleeve, and cut out.

07 Decorate the front of the envelope sleeves with the bride and groom's initials. Add a decorative motif to the larger envelope sleeve (we have used a printed heart). Concertina-fold the date pennants together and place them into the smaller (right-hand) envelope sleeve. Slip the smaller envelope sleeve into the larger (left-hand) sleeve.

BUTTON STEM
BRIDAL BOUQUET

USE VINTAGE AND MODERN BUTTONS TO CREATE A RAINBOW-COLOURED WEDDING BOUQUET. INDIVIDUAL 'FLOWER' STEMS ARE MADE FROM STACKED BUTTONS, WHICH ARE THEN GATHERED TOGETHER TO MAKE A SIMPLE YET STUNNING POSY MEASURING APPROX 20CM (8IN) HIGH x 15CM (6IN) WIDE FOR A LASTING WEDDING DAY MEMENTO.

EVERLASTING
FLOWERS

HOW TO MAKE... BRIDAL BOUQUET

MATERIALS

APPROX 250 BUTTONS

70 PIECES OF GREEN FLORAL WIRE EACH MEASURING APPROX 30cm (12in)

1m (1⅛yd) OF 2.5cm- (1in-) WIDE GREEN GROSGRAIN RIBBON

GREEN FLORAL TAPE

PAIR OF PLIERS

FABRIC GLUE

TIP

Source buttons from craft fairs, haberdashery shops and vintage markets, and ask your granny if you can raid her button tin.

01 Gather together a large collection of rainbow-coloured buttons. You should choose as wide a variety as you can, from solid plastic to translucent glass, and try to find some buttons that have interesting textures or novelty shapes. You will need a good selection of buttons in terms of their size and shape.

02 Start to stack your buttons together to give interesting colour combinations, making sure to place the smallest buttons on the top of each stack. Use two, three or four buttons for each button flower. You will need about 70 button stacks, and do try to make these as varied as possible.

03 Take a piece of the floral wire and fold it in half to make a loop. Thread one of your button stacks onto the wire loop. Hold the wire firmly as you thread the buttons all the way to the end of the loop.

04 Twist the wire to hold the buttons firmly in place, using pliers to tighten if necessary. Continue to thread each button stack onto each piece of floral wire to make a total of 70 button flower stems. For the neatest finish, wrap each individual stem with green floral tape to hide the twisted wires – this has the added advantage of making the stems stronger so that they are less prone to bend out of shape.

05 Now begin to arrange the button flower stems together to make your bouquet, working in much the same way as you would to make a floral bouquet, adding each stem one at a time and checking the shape of the bouquet as you go. Make sure you place contrasting buttons next to each other to add interest.

06 Once you are happy with the bouquet's shape, secure the stems together with floral tape to form the bouquet handle. Take the green ribbon and, starting at the bottom of the stems, begin to wrap the ribbon around the handle. If necessary you can secure the ribbon in place as you go with fabric glue. When you reach the top of the handle, trim off any excess ribbon leaving just enough to tuck in at the top; secure the tucked-in ribbon end with fabric glue.

01

02

EMMA LYTH aka BEAUBUTTONS

Emma spends her days feeding her button obsession by meticulously sourcing beautiful, quirky and unusual buttons to use in her renowned bouquet creations. An industry expert in alternative bridal bouquets with a natural eye for design and composition, Emma is inspired by the fabulous 1950s, with a penchant for all things kitsch. See more of her designs online at www.beaubuttons.co.uk

03

05

TIP

One large spool of floral tape should be sufficient for a small bouquet, to neaten the wired stems and to help keep the bouquet's shape.

06

BLACKBOARD FEATHER
NAPKIN RINGS

DECORATE YOUR PLACE SETTINGS WITH THESE SIMPLE BUT SMART NAPKIN RINGS. THE COLOURS CAN BE MATCHED TO YOUR WEDDING THEME, AND THE CARDBOARD FEATHERS ARE COVERED WITH BLACKBOARD PAINT, SO THEY DOUBLE UP AS PLACE CARDS TOO. INVITE YOUR GUESTS TO TAKE THEM HOME AS A REMINDER OF THE DAY.

TABLE
PLACE-MARKER

anna

paul

Boris

Marina

HOW TO MAKE... NAPKIN RINGS

SEE P90 FOR TEMPLATE

MATERIALS

COTTON FABRIC: APPROX 6 x 20cm (2⅜ x 8in) PER NAPKIN RING

PATTERNED SCRAPBOOKING PAPER

CARD: FLEXIBLE FOR THE NAPKIN RING AND STIFF FOR THE FEATHER

THIN COLOURED CARD FOR THE NAPKIN RING BACKING

METALLIC EMBROIDERY THREAD

EYELETS AND EYELET SETTER

BLACKBOARD PAINT AND SMALL PAINTBRUSH

PENCIL AND RULER

CUTTING MAT, CRAFT KNIFE AND SCISSORS

GLUE STICK AND HOLE PUNCH

CHALK OR CHALK MARKER

01 Cut a strip of flexible card measuring 3.5 x 17cm (1⅜ x 6¾in), then cut a piece of your cotton fabric approx 1cm (⅜in) larger all the way around. Cover one side of the card with glue and place it sticky-side down onto the wrong side of the fabric, positioning it centrally. Spread more glue over the other side of the card, and then fold the fabric corners over diagonally, pressing down firmly onto the adhesive.

02 Fold the fabric over each of the four edges, again pressing down firmly onto the card strip. Choose a thin coloured card to co-ordinate with your napkin fabric and cut a strip from it measuring approx 3 x 16cm (1⅛ x 6¼in). Glue the strip of coloured card to the back of the fabric-covered card to hide the raw edges of the fabric.

03 Curve the ends of the covered strip around so that they overlap by 1cm (⅜in), and punch a hole through both ends where they overlap. Feed an eyelet through the holes, and squeeze it shut with the eyelet setter, to hold the ring in place (alternatively, use a paper fastener).

04 Trace the feather template onto patterned paper and cut out. Trace a second feather onto thick card and carefully cut out using a craft knife, working on a cutting mat to protect your work surface.

05 Paint the cardboard feather with one or two coats of blackboard paint, and set aside to dry. (For an extra-neat finish, you can also paint the back of the cardboard feather, choosing a colour to co-ordinate with the fabric.)

06 Cut a length of metallic thread measuring approx 30cm (12in) long. Hold the two feathers together over the front of the ring (patterned paper and blackboard sides facing up) and tie in place with the thread. Finally, use a chalk marker to add the name of your guest to the blackboard feather.

TIP

To use recycled materials, breakfast cereal box card is the perfect weight for making the rings, and the feathers can be cut from board-backed envelopes.

01

02

KIRSTY NEALE

Kirsty is a freelance writer and designer-maker. She specialises in fabric and paper projects and enjoys combining new materials with vintage or repurposed finds. Her work has been published in numerous books and magazines, and she blogs at www.kirstyneale.typepad.com

03

04

05

06

FELT CUTWORK
LANTERN WRAPS

USE GLASS PAINT AND SIMPLE STITCHED BANDS OF FELT TO TRANSFORM GLASS JARS INTO COLOURFUL LANTERNS. A GROUP OF THREE MAKES A WONDERFUL WAY TO LIGHT UP THE CENTRE OF EACH GUEST TABLE AT THE WEDDING RECEPTION. FOR SAFETY'S SAKE, THESE LANTERNS SHOULD ONLY BE USED WITH BATTERY-OPERATED TEA-LIGHTS.

DRESS UP YOUR GLASS JARS

HOW TO MAKE... LANTERN WRAPS

MATERIALS

THREE CLEAN GLASS JARS PER GUEST TABLE

FELT: RED, ORANGE AND TURQUOISE

EMBROIDERY THREADS: RED, ORANGE AND TURQUOISE

PEBEO VITREA 160 GLASS PAINT: PEPPER RED, PAPRIKA AND TURQUOISE

ASSORTED GLASS BEADS IN RED, ORANGE AND TURQUOISE

CRAFT WIRE APPROX 20 GAUGE

SCISSORS, THIN CARD, PENCIL AND PAPER

TAPE MEASURE, BALLPOINT PEN AND TRANSPARENT RULER

EMBROIDERY SCISSORS, EMBROIDERY NEEDLE, PAPER CLIPS AND PINS

SMOOTH MAKE-UP SPONGES AND PAINT TRAY

BAKING TRAY AND FOIL

PAIR OF PLIERS AND WIRE CUTTERS

01 Trace off the butterfly and heart templates and transfer onto thin card. Make a wrap template from paper, measuring it to the jar circumference plus a 2cm (¾in) overlap. Use the wrap template to cut out three felt rectangles, one from each colour.

02 Use the heart and butterfly templates and a ballpoint pen to mark out the cutwork design onto the felt rectangles starting in the middle, using a transparent ruler to keep the design level. Use embroidery scissors to make a small V-shaped cut in the middle of each shape, and cut outwards to carefully follow the marked outlines.

03 Use three strands of contrasting thread to sew a line of running stitch around the large heart and along the top and bottom edges.

04 Wrap the felt around the jar and use paper clips to hold the ends together. Carefully slide the wrap off, pin, then secure with a line of running stitches.

05 To paint the jars, place one hand inside the jar and apply the paint with your other hand. Dab the make-up sponge in the glass paint, wiping off the excess onto the edge of the paint tray. Apply the paint in smooth, fast strokes, covering the base first, then painting the sides, spreading it thinly for a tinted effect. Use long vertical strokes starting just under the rim and finishing at the base, leaving the rims unpainted. Leave the jars to dry upside down for a minimum of 24 hours.

LAURA HOWARD aka LUPIN

Laura is a not-quite grown up girl who likes to make and do and is completely obsessed with felt. She shares free tutorials and writes about her crafty adventures on her blog bugsandfishes.blogspot.com and sells her work at www.lupin.bigcartel.com

SEE P90 FOR TEMPLATES

06 Put the jars right side up on a foil-covered baking tray, place in an oven set to 160ºC (325ºF) and bake for 40 minutes. Leave to cool completely before removing.

07 Make a wire handle to fit each jar. Cut one piece of wire to sit just under the rim, wrapping it around twice, allowing a few centimetres (1–2in) extra at each end. Cut a second piece of wire for the handle itself, making an upside down U-shape, again allowing a little extra.

08 Bend one end of the handle upwards. Thread on some glass beads at the other end, then bend upwards too. Hook the beaded handle onto the wire circle; carefully place the circle under the rim. Pull the circle tight, and twist the ends together to secure.

09 Adjust the position of the handle, then wrap the ends around it to hold it in place. Trim excess wire and bend the wire ends neatly in place. Slip the felt wraps onto the jars.

EXPRESS YOURSELF
PLACE SETTING

UNLEASH YOUR GUESTS' CREATIVITY AT YOUR WEDDING RECEPTION. MAKE EACH PLACE SETTING A FRAMED SPACE IN WHICH THEY CAN RECORD THEIR THOUGHTS OF YOUR SPECIAL DAY IN WORDS AND PICTURES, FROM HEARTFELT MESSAGES TO CARTOON SKETCHES. COVER POTS WITH PRETTY PATTERNED PAPERS, FILL WITH PENCILS AND LEAVE IN THE CENTRE OF EACH TABLE.

HOW TO MAKE... PLACE SETTING

SEE P90 FOR TEMPLATES

MATERIALS

ONE ROLL OF PATTERNED WALLPAPER

ONE ROLL OF THICK LINING PAPER

SELECTION OF PATTERNED PAPERS TO COVER POTS AND PENCILS

POTS AND PENCILS FOR COVERING

CLIP PHOTO STANDS

TRACING PAPER AND PENCILS (HB AND 2H)

CUTTING MAT, CRAFT KNIFE AND METAL RULER

NUMBER RUBBER STAMPS AND INK PAD

SCISSORS AND GLUE

TIP

Pretty wallpaper samples are perfect for making the frames, and small scraps of craft or wrapping paper are ideal for covering the pots and pencils. Smooth round pencils are easiest to cover.

01 To make the frame, cut a rectangle from the patterned paper measuring 38 x 32cm (15 x 12½in). Fold it in half with right sides facing, then fold in half again. Use a soft HB pencil to trace the large frame template. Turn the tracing paper over and place the two straight edges on the folded edges of the paper. Use the harder 2H pencil to go over the tracing.

02 Cut out the shape using scissors around the shaped sections, and the metal ruler and craft knife for the straight lines. Open out the frame. Iron out the crease line to make the paper completely flat if you wish.

03 Cut out a rectangle from the lining paper measuring 17 x 29cm (6¾ x 11⅜in). Glue around the inside edge of the lining paper rectangle, place the cut out frame over the lining paper and press down all around the edge to secure.

04 To make the small frame for the guest table number, follow steps 1 and 2, using the small frame template. Apply glue to the back of the patterned paper frame and stick it down onto a piece of lining paper cut larger than the frame. Use scissors to cut out around the shape

of the frame. Working in this way makes the frame a little stronger, and this will prevent it from bending when you put it in the clip photo stand. Use the number stamps to print the guest table number in the middle of the frame.

05 Cut out a piece of paper to cover the pot: this should be a rectangle that is the same height as the pot, which can be wrapped around the pot with an overlap of approx 2cm (¾in). Apply glue to the inside edge of the overlap. Wrap the paper around the pot and press the glued edge down firmly.

06 Cut out a piece of paper to cover a pencil: this should be a rectangle that is the same length as the pencil up to the start of the pointed end, which can be wrapped around the pencil with an overlap of approx 1cm (⅜in). Apply glue to the inside edge of the overlap, wrap the paper tightly around the pencil and press the glued edge down firmly.

DESIGNED
BY CLARE
YOUNGS

TIP

Don't forget to delegate
the job of collecting up
the mats at the end of
the day.

CROSS STITCH

WEDDING SAMPLER

COMMEMORATE THE BIG DAY WITH THIS STYLISH MODERN TAKE ON THE TRADITIONAL SAMPLER. FITTING INTO A STANDARD PHOTO FRAME, THE DESIGN CAN BE PERSONALISED TO MAKE A FUTURE HEIRLOOM THAT WILL BE TREASURED FOR YEARS TO COME. THIS PROJECT IS PERFECT FOR BEGINNERS WITH AN ITCH TO STITCH AS THERE IS NO COMPLICATED MAKING UP.

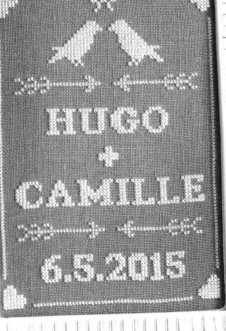

HUGO
+
CAMILLE
6.5.2015

POLAROID
Land Camera
Model 160
MADE IN

HOW TO MAKE... WEDDING SAMPLER

MATERIALS

ONE PIECE OF 32-COUNT MOCHA LINEN OR EVENWEAVE FABRIC (OR 16-COUNT AIDA) MEASURING 20 x 20CM (8 x 8IN)

EMBROIDERY THREADS:
CREAM x 4M (ANCHOR 926/DMC 712);
PALE PEACH x 2M (ANCHOR 366/DMC 739)

STANDARD PHOTO FRAME 12.5 x 18CM (5 x 7IN) (GLASS OPTIONAL)

MOUNT BACKING BOARD AND MASKING TAPE

USE OF PHOTOCOPIER, PAPER, SCISSORS AND GLUE FOR PERSONALISING PATTERN

TAPESTRY NEEDLE SIZE 24 OR 26

MINI NO-SEW ROLLER FRAME 23 x 15CM (9 x 6IN) OR EMBROIDERY HOOP APPROX 20CM (8IN) (OPTIONAL)

SMALL PAIR OF EMBROIDERY SCISSORS

CUTTING MAT, CRAFT KNIFE AND METAL RULER

IRON AND TOWEL

01 Photocopy (or scan and print) the wedding sampler chart and the alphabet chart. Cut out the letters and numbers you need, arrange them in the shaded areas on the chart and glue in place, taking care to match up the grid squares.

02 Take your fabric and find its centre by folding it in half horizontally and then vertically. These fold lines correspond to the arrows marked at the side of the charted designs (indicating the chart centre) and will ensure that you work your design centrally on the fabric. Mark the centre point with a pin or needle, and place the fabric in the embroidery frame or hoop.

03 Cut a length of embroidery thread, separate a single strand, fold it in half and thread the ends through the tapestry needle. When making your first half stitch, leave a few centimetres (couple of inches) of thread at the back of the fabric (the end with the loop), then pass the needle and thread through the loop and pull closed to secure the thread without a knot.

SOPHIE SIMPSON
aka WHAT DELILAH DID

Sophie is the designer, writer and compulsive stitcher behind embroidery business, What Delilah Did. A perpetual dreamer and period-drama obsessive, she most ardently wishes she'd been born centuries ago. Her first book *Storyland Cross Stitch* has recently been published.
www.whatdelilahdid.com

SEE P94 FOR CHARTS

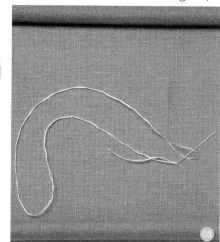

04 Working in sections from the centre upwards, stitch your personalised pattern. Each cross is stitched over two threads on linen or evenweave (see Charts, p94, for instructions for working cross stitches). If working on 16-count aida, make each stitch over one block.

05 When the top half is complete, turn the frame upside down and stitch the rest of the pattern in sections from the centre as before.

06 Remove the fabric from the frame and hand wash if necessary. Iron the embroidery face down over a towel to protect the stitches.

07 Measure and cut a piece of mount backing board just slightly smaller than your photo frame. Neatly stretch and fold the fabric around the board, tape into place and insert into the frame.

FLOWER INSPIRATIONS

BEAUTIFUL BOUQUETS

01

Autumn Davidson of Autumn & Grace Bridal is a fabric florist specialising in repurposing vintage materials into memorable and personal heirloom bouquets. This tea-stained fabric bouquet (photographed by Aaron Wilcox) features vintage-garden hues, touches of satin greenery and lace. To see more of her work, visit www.autumnandgracebridal.com

02

This stunning bouquet by Noaki Schwartz (photographed by Yuna Leonard) features a mix of red rhinestone jewellery set in gold and millinery roses against a bed of ivory cloth flowers. Pearls and faceted glass beads have been wired into the arrangement for added texture, and rhinestones set on the petals of the cloth flowers for a bit more sparkle. www.noakijewelry.com

03

Debbie Carlisle uses vintage buttons, jewellery, beads and fabrics to create luxurious bespoke bridal bouquets for brides to treasure forever. Her hand-crafted heirloom designs come in every colour of the rainbow. This small purple button posy works beautifully with a slim line or tea length prom-style wedding gown. www.dcbouquets.co.uk

BLOOMING LOVELY

04

Lindy Blake Miller of Atlanta, Georgia makes exquisite vintage-book bouquets and corsages. The idea first came to her when she found a 100-year-old book destined for destruction and thought it would make a perfect 'something old' for a bride's 'something new', and so she began harvesting printed history for exceptional brides to be.
www.theepapergirl.etsy.com

05

A vintage jewellery corsage or buttonhole makes a lovely alternative to flowers and doubles as a gift to keep as a lasting reminder of your big day. Debbie Carlisle uses tiny vintage buttons, beads and crystals to create her buttonholes, and each design is unique.
www.dcbouquets.co.uk

06

Natural earthy hues are a great choice for the groomsmen's boutonnieres. Designed by Donni of Fairyfolk Weddings, the spring boutonniere combines natural feathers with vintage paper roses, and is wrapped in natural twine with a country check bow to finish. For more of Donni's whimsical designs visit
www.FairyfolkWeddings.etsy.com

FUN TO SEW
TRUE LOVE CUSHIONS

THESE PERSONALISED CUSHIONS ARE A GREAT WAY TO SEAT BRIDE AND GROOM IN COMFORT AND STYLE. LEATHER HEART APPLIQUÉS, INSPIRED BY 1950S ROCKABILLY TATTOOS, ARE TEAMED UP WITH CUTE POLKA DOTS AND POM-POMS. FOR A NAUTICAL FEEL, USE STRIPED FABRIC AND A GOLD ANCHOR MOTIF INSTEAD.

LUCA

CLAUDIA

TOP TABLE GLAMOUR

HOW TO MAKE... TRUE LOVE CUSHIONS

MATERIALS (PER PAIR)

LEATHER: ONE PIECE OF RED MEASURING 20 x 20CM (8 x 8IN), ONE PIECE OF WHITE MEASURING 20 x 16CM (8 x 6¼IN) AND ONE PIECE OF BLACK MEASURING 6 x 20CM (2⅜ x 8IN)

1M (1⅛YD) OF POLKA-DOT FABRIC

3M (3¼YD) OF POM-POM TRIM

BLACK EMBROIDERY THREAD

SEWING THREAD

TWO CUSHION PADS MEASURING 35 x 35CM (14 x 14IN)

FABRIC GLUE

LEATHER NEEDLE, PINS AND SCISSORS

SEWING MACHINE AND IRON

TIP
Always use a leather needle when sewing leather – it has a triangular tip which helps the needle to glide easily through, making it so much easier to sew with. A thimble may also help.

01 Using the templates provided and working on the suede side of the leather, cut out the heart shape from red leather, and the scroll and two scroll ends from white leather.

02 Cut out the letters for the bride's name from a long strip of black leather 3cm (1⅛in) high. Draw the outline of your letters IN REVERSE on the suede side of the leather, so that they will read the right way round. You may find it helpful to write them onto tracing paper first, then flip the tracing over to copy the name onto the suede.

03 Glue the cut out letters onto the leather side of the scroll. Using a leather needle and black embroidery thread, hand stitch the letters in place, making sure that the corners in particular are securely stitched.

04 Now glue the scroll onto the leather side of the heart. Arrange the scroll ends and glue in place on the underside of the heart. Hand stitch all of the pieces into place with neat, straight stitches.

05 From the polka-dot fabric, cut one piece measuring 37cm (14½in) square, and two rectangles measuring 20 x 37cm (8 x 14½in) and 26 x 37cm (10¼ x 14½in). Attach the leather heart in the centre of the fabric square using a little glue, and hand stitch in place.

06 Cut four 37cm (14½in) lengths of pom-pom trim and pin around the edges of the fabric square, with the pom-poms facing inwards. Machine stitch using a small zigzag stitch.

ZOE LARKINS

Zoe Larkins is the inspired designer-maker behind accessories label Love From Hetty & Dave, and she is most often to be found busily stitching away in her shop/ studio in Bournemouth on the south coast of England.
For more about her work, visit www.lovefromhettyanddave.co.uk

SEE P91 FOR TEMPLATES

01

03

07 Use the polka-dot fabric rectangles to make an envelope opening cushion back. Prepare each rectangle by folding one long edge under by 6mm (¼in), then fold over again by 1cm (⅜in); press, pin and machine stitch to complete the hemming.

08 Lay the heart appliqué right side up on your work surface. Place the smaller hemmed rectangle on top, right side facing down with raw edges aligning at the top and sides. Now position the larger hemmed rectangle to align the raw edges at the bottom and sides, so that it overlaps the smaller hemmed rectangle. Pin in place. Machine stitch slowly around the edges to avoid catching the pom-poms under the needle, carefully pushing them in as you sew if necessary.

09 Carefully snip off the corners and turn right side out. Use the point of your scissors to gently push out the corners before inserting the cushion pad. Now make a second cushion for the groom.

04

06

07

08

KOKESHI-STYLE
WEDDING DECORATION

MADE FROM EASY-TO-MOULD POLYMER CLAY, THIS TINY KOKESHI COUPLE CAN BE CUSTOMISED TO RESEMBLE ANY BRIDE AND GROOM. MAKE THEM A FAUX-WOODEN DANCE FLOOR, COMPLETE WITH CONFETTI AND A STRING OF HEARTS, AND THEY'RE READY TO TAKE UP POSITION ON THE TOP TIER OF YOUR CAKE OR IN THE MIDDLE OF THE TOP TABLE.

EASY TO CUSTOMISE

HOW TO MAKE... WEDDING DECORATION

SEE P91 FOR TEMPLATES

MATERIALS

OVEN-BAKE MODELLING POLYMER CLAY

ACRYLIC PAINT: BLACK, WHITE, PINK AND SUITABLE COLOURS FOR HAIR AND SKIN TONES

FINE BLACK MARKER PEN

SMALL SCRAPS OF PATTERNED AND WHITE PAPER

WOODGRAIN-PATTERNED PAPER

SMALL SCRAPS OF WHITE COTTON FABRIC AND SCALLOPED-EDGED LACE

SMALL EMBELLISHMENTS: PAPER OR FABRIC FLOWERS, AND SEED BEADS

TWO BAMBOO SKEWERS

KITCHEN SCALES, ROLLING PIN AND BAKING SHEET

COTTON BUD, SMALL PAINTBRUSH, PENCIL, PVA GLUE AND SCISSORS

ELASTIC BAND AND COCKTAIL STICKS

NEEDLE AND WHITE EMBROIDERY THREAD

HOLE PUNCH AND SMALL HEART PUNCH

01 For each figure, take three pieces of clay weighing approx 25g (just under an ounce), 30g (just over an ounce) and 5g (small piece). Roll the largest piece into a cone shape approx 5cm (2in) tall, and the other two into round balls. Flatten the smallest ball into a disc shape.

02 Press the disc onto the bottom of the cone. Gently push a cocktail stick partway down into the cone. Add the head on top, so the cocktail stick is completely hidden, and the head and body are securely joined together.

03 For the bride, roll another small ball of clay (approx 5g) to make the bun for her hair. Break off a small piece of cocktail stick, and push one end into the ball. Push the other end into the side of the head. Bake the clay figures according to the manufacturer's instructions.

TIP

If the head and body become separated after baking, add a little PVA glue to the cocktail stick and the surface of the clay, press the join together firmly and leave to dry before painting.

04 Paint the head and the neck and upper body of each figure using an appropriate flesh tone. Paint on the bride's dress and the groom's shirt in white, and use black for the groom's trousers.

05 Use a pencil to lightly draw on the facial features and a hairline. Trace over the facial features with a fine black marker pen. Use the end of a cocktail stick to add a tiny dot of white paint to each eye, and a cotton bud to add dots of pink for the cheeks. Paint on the hair using an appropriate colour. For variations on hair and facial details see p41.

06 To dress the groom, use the templates provided to cut a collar from white paper and a tie and waistcoat from patterned paper. Spread glue over the back of the waistcoat and wrap around the body, using an elastic band to hold it in place while the glue dries. Stick on the collar and tie, and add a small paper or fabric flower for the boutonniere.

TIP

Each rolled figure will be a slightly different size and shape, so you might need to make one or two small adjustments before cutting out the groom's waistcoat. Copy it first onto scrap paper and wrap it around the body to check that it fits.

HOW TO MAKE... WEDDING DECORATION (CONTINUED)

07 To dress the bride, cut a 4 x 15cm (1½ x 6in) strip of white fabric. Fold over a narrow hem along the bottom edge and sew into place with running stitch, adding a single seed bead to each stitch. Sew a gathering stitch around the top edge of the skirt. Place the skirt around the bride's waist, pull the thread ends taut, then knot together.

08 Spread a thin layer of glue over the upper half of the bride's body and the top of her skirt. Cut a piece of scalloped-edged lace, lining it up in the centre of the bride's torso for the sweetheart neckline. Press it down firmly and add a few stitches at the back to hold the ends securely together. Glue a paper flower to the bride's bun to finish.

09 To make the base, roll out a circle of clay approx 12.5cm (5in) in diameter and 6mm (¼in) thick. Use a bamboo skewer to make a hole approx 1cm (⅜in) in from the edge at either side. Bake, and once the disc has completely cooled, cut out a circle of woodgrain-patterned paper and glue on top, re-marking the skewer holes.

10 Hole punch through coloured paper to make tiny pieces of confetti. Place the bride and groom figures in the centre of the base, then sprinkle confetti randomly around them. Lift the figures away, and glue the confetti into place.

11 To make the banner, punch out five or six heart shapes from patterned paper. Cut a 50cm (20in) length of white embroidery thread, and use a needle to thread it through the top edges of each heart.

12 Snip the pointed ends off two bamboo sticks, so that each measures approx 17cm (6¾in) tall. Push the skewers into the holes in the base. Tie on the heart banner adding a little glue over the knots, then trim the thread ends to the desired length. Finally, glue the bride and groom to the base, positioning them so that they are facing slightly towards each other.

HOW TO MAKE... VARIATIONS

Give the groom a beard.

Add details to match
your bridal accessories.

Add a wavy or scalloped edge
to suggest curly hair.

Use a length of fancy braid or trim
to make a headdress.

Add extra balls of clay
to make a piled-high hairstyle.

Make a tiara from crystal
and pearl beads.

To make a pair of glasses, cut two 17cm (6¾in) lengths of jewellery wire. Twist them together in the centre, then use pliers to bend the pieces on either side into rectangles (right). Twist the wires together again at the outer edge of each rectangle, and snip off any excess. Bend the twisted ends so that they are at right angles to the frames to make arms (far right). Add a small amount of glue to the back of each arm and the twisted centre section before pressing the glasses into place on the head.

FOLDED FABRIC
CORSAGES & BOUTONNIERES

A WEDDING WOULDN'T BE A WEDDING WITHOUT AN ARRAY OF BEAUTIFUL BLOOMS. NOW YOU CAN BECOME YOUR OWN FABRIC FLORIST BY MAKING THESE BEAUTIFUL VINTAGE-STYLE CORSAGES AND BOUTONNIERES FOR ALL YOUR GUESTS. GORGEOUS ON THE DAY, THEY MAKE A LASTING SOUVENIR TO TAKE HOME.

VINTAGE
STYLE

HOW TO MAKE... CORSAGES & BOUTONNIERES

SEE P91 FOR TEMPLATES

MATERIALS

TONING SMALL-PRINT FABRICS OF YOUR CHOICE

SEWING THREADS TO MATCH

DOUBLE-SIDED FUSIBLE WEBBING

STIFF WIRE FOR FLOWER STEMS AND DECORATIVE CRAFT WIRE FOR LEAF STEMS

RIBBON

SEWING NEEDLE

PINKING SHEARS, DRESSMAKER'S SCISSORS AND SCISSORS FOR CUTTING WIRE

SAFETY PINS AND FANCY-HEADED PINS

TIP

To make the flower for each corsage or boutonniere, you will need two toning small-print fabrics each measuring approx 35 x 35cm (14 x 14in), as well as a little green fabric for the leaves. Cutting on the bias gives the petal shapes a little bit of stretch for a lovely curvy look.

01 Start by making a corsage. Fuse your chosen fabrics together with fusible webbing. Use the petal templates to cut seven small petals and eight large petals on the bias by placing templates diagonally on the fabric. Cut a 2 x 30cm (¾ x 12in) fabric strip also on the bias.

02 Snip into the centre of each petal. Gently fray the edges by using a pin to pull some of the threads free. Screw up into a tight ball and roll between your fingers. Open out, hold the corners and tug. Repeat along one long edge of the fabric strip.

03 To make the flower centre, roll one end of the fabric strip to give you a tight start, then work outwards, coiling and twisting the fabric as you go. Tuck the loose end underneath and secure with a few stitches.

04 Add the smaller petals first. Overlap the slit fabric at the petal base for a curved shape and stitch to the back of the flower centre. Add the next petal slightly overlapping the first, repeating to add all the small petals.

05 Attach the outer row of eight large petals as step 4. Use pinking shears to cut two large leaves from green fabric; fold in half and press the 'vein' lines. Snip into the centre at the base, overlap and attach to the flower back. Sew a fabric circle over the back to fix a safety pin to.

JENNY DIXON

A craft journalist by trade, Jenny has always loved to make things. She is based in Bath in the UK, where she shares her home with an outrageously large fabric stash. Find her online at:
www.jennysbuttonjar.wordpress.com

06 To make a boutonniere, fuse fabrics together and cut out five large petals and a 4 x 30cm (1½ x 12in) fabric strip, all on the bias. Gather the fabric strip to make the flower centre: work small running stitches along one edge and pull tight. Start by rolling the strip tightly, then a little more loosely, until you reach the end; stitch through the base of the coil to secure.

07 Add each of the large petals in turn around the flower centre: keep them close and upright, and overlap as you go. (To give a more realistic look, roll the top edge of the petals and crease with your fingernail to hold in place.) Cut a piece of wire for the stem and push it into the base. Cut a 4cm (1½in) fabric circle and make a snip to the centre. Fit the fabric circle around the stem and fold into a cone shape to fit neatly around the base of the flower, then stitch it in place.

08 Use pinking shears to cut three small leaves from bonded fabrics. Take a length of decorative craft wire, double it, twist it and stitch it to the front of one of the leaves to create a central vein and stem. Repeat for the other two leaves, then twist the stems of all the leaves together to create the spray. Place the spray behind the flower and bind all the stems together tightly with ribbon, stitching the end to fasten. Use fancy-headed pins to attach the boutonnieres.

CUT AND PRINT

WEDDING INVITES

USE SIMPLE PAPER CUTTING AND LINO-PRINTING TECHNIQUES TO CREATE PERSONALISED, HAND-CRAFTED WEDDING INVITATIONS INSPIRED BY POLISH PAPER CUTS AND FOLK ART DESIGNS. THERE ARE TWO DESIGNS FOR YOU TO CHOOSE FROM, AND EACH CAN BE EASILY CUSTOMISED WITH YOUR OWN INITIALS.

HANDMADE
INVITATIONS

HOW TO MAKE... WEDDING INVITES

MATERIALS

PIECES OF WHITE CARD
MEASURING 15 x 30cm (6 x 12in)

PIECES OF COLOURED PAPER
MEASURING 15 x 15cm (6 x 6in)

SPEEDY CARVE LINO BLOCK
AND LINO CUTTER

INK PADS IN COLOURS OF YOUR CHOOSING

LINO ROLLER OR BRAYER

MINIATURE HEART PUNCH

TRACING PAPER, PENCIL AND ERASER

CUTTING MAT, CRAFT KNIFE AND
METAL RULER

TIP
To make it easier to grip your stamp when printing, you can mount it onto a wood block using very strong glue.

01 To make the heart wreath invite, fold a piece of white card in half. Make a tracing of the heart wreath template, filling in all the leaves as solid shapes. Transfer the design onto the front of the folded card with the fold at the top.

02 Open the card out flat on the cutting mat. Use a craft knife to carefully cut away all of the areas of the heart design shaded in pencil, making sure to leave gaps in the design as marked on the template: these strengthen the card to prevent it from flopping over when standing. Erase any remaining pencil marks, and glue a square of coloured paper to the inside back of the card.

03 Make a lino-cut stamp of the bride and groom's initials. Transfer your design onto a small rectangle of speedy carve lino block, using your fingernail to rub the traced image on. Your letters should appear reversed and mirrored so that they will print the right way around.

04 Use the lino cutter to carefully cut away all the areas that you do not want to print, leaving the pencil lines uncut to form your stamp.

05 Make a test print: press the ink pad firmly over the stamp, and use a lino roller or brayer over the back of the stamp to achieve an even print. Make any adjustments to your stamp before using it to print the initials in the centre of the paper-cut heart.

SEE P91 FOR TEMPLATES

06 To make the bird invite, take a piece of white card, mark the midway point on each long side and fold the edges into the centre to give you a gatefold card.

07 Use the bird template to trace the bird design (one in reverse) onto two small squares of lino block. Personalise the bird stamps with the bride and groom's initials, remembering to reverse letters as necessary so they read correctly when printed. Use the lino cutter to cut away all the areas that you don't want to print and trim away any excess from the outer edge of the design.

08 Make a test print before using the finished stamps to print the birds facing each other, one on each side of the front of the gatefold card.

09 Open the card out flat and punch out a heart border along the top and bottom edges of the gatefold. Refold and glue a coloured paper square to the centre panel of the inside of the card.

ZEENA SHAH

Zeena Shah studied printed textile design at Chelsea School of Art & Design and has since worked in both the fashion and interiors textile industry before launching her own label, z e e n a – a collection of hand silk screen printed and handmade textiles for the home.
www.zeenashah.com

FELT APPLIQUÉ
RING PILLOW

INSPIRED BY BRIGHT FLORAL PRINTS OF THE 1960S AND 1970S, THIS SMALL PILLOW
MEASURING 18CM (7IN) SQUARE AND DECORATED WITH A PROFUSION OF COLOURFUL FELT
FLOWERS AND SPARKLY SEED BEADS IS PERFECT FOR KEEPING YOUR WEDDING RINGS SAFE ON
YOUR BIG DAY. IT HAS A USEFUL CARRYING STRAP ON THE BACK FOR LITTLE HANDS.

KEEPSAKE
CUSHION

HOW TO MAKE... RING PILLOW

SEE P92 FOR TEMPLATES

MATERIALS

ONE PIECE OF IVORY FELT
MEASURING 26 x 37cm (10¼ x 14½in)

ONE PIECE EACH OF ORANGE,
SATSUMA, YELLOW, CORAL, CANDY PINK
AND PALE PINK FELT MEASURING
APPROX 11 x 17cm (4¼ x 6¾in)

ONE PIECE OF PEACH FELT
MEASURING APPROX 9 x 14cm (3½ x 5½in)

ONE PIECE OF BRIGHT PINK FELT
MEASURING APPROX 14 x 16cm (5½ x 6¼in)

SEWING THREADS TO MATCH FELT COLOURS

EMBROIDERY THREADS: CORAL, ORANGE,
YELLOW, PALE PINK AND BRIGHT PINK

SEED BEADS IN MATCHING COLOURS
(SIZE 8/0)

APPROX 26cm (10¼in) OF NARROW
LIGHT PINK RIBBON

POLYESTER STUFFING

SCISSORS, EMBROIDERY SCISSORS,
NEEDLES AND PINS

01 Use the templates provided to cut out all the flower pieces marked A–E in the quantities and colours marked on the templates. From the ivory felt, cut out two 18cm (7in) squares for the pillow front and back, and a rectangle measuring 6.5 x 12.5cm (2½ x 5in) for the carry strap.

02 Take one of the ivory felt squares and place pieces 1 and 2 of flowers A–D as shown in the photo, with the flowers slightly overhanging at the edges. Using double thickness ivory sewing thread, sew a small cross stitch in the centre of each flower.

03 Using three strands of the embroidery thread (coral for flower A, yellow for B, bright pink for C and orange for D), sew lines of running stitch radiating from the centre of each flower.

04 Sew pieces 1 and 2 of flower E in the pillow centre, adding lines of pale pink running stitch as in the photo. Now add pieces A3, B3, C3 and D3, sewing on with matching sewing thread.

05 Cut out small flowers and circles in assorted colours to fill in the gaps between the large flowers.

06 Add the remaining pieces E3 and E4 to the central flower, and sew a line of running stitch around the centre circle with matching sewing thread.

07 To embellish the corner flowers, sew clusters of seed beads, starting in the middle and working outwards in circles. Sew each bead in position with a double thickness of sewing thread to match the bead colour. Add a single seed bead to the infill flowers and circles. Sew the midpoint of the ribbon to the centre of the pillow, having trimmed the ribbon ends at an angle to help prevent fraying.

TIP

For the precise cutting of the felt flowers, use embroidery scissors: it may help to use transparent parcel tape rather than pins to fix the paper templates to the felt.

08 To make the carrying strap, pin the felt rectangle in the centre of the undecorated ivory square and stitch one or two lines of backstitch along each of the short ends. Remove pins.

09 Place the pillow front and back together with right sides facing out, and pin. The top (front) square may have shrunk slightly from the appliqué stitching, so if necessary trim any excess felt from the bottom (back) square so that back and front match exactly. Blanket stitch together, folding the flower petals out of the way as you sew past them, and leaving a small gap for stuffing.

10 Stuff the pillow gradually with small pieces of stuffing for an even finish, then blanket stitch the opening closed.

DESIGNED
BY LAURA
HOWARD

CARVED HEARTS
TABLE CENTREPIECE

THIS NATURE-THEMED TABLE SETTING MAKES GREAT USE OF NATURAL MATERIALS LIKE THE STACKED LOGS, WHILE THE TABLE NUMBER AND THE BRIDE AND GROOM'S INITIALS ARE 'CARVED' INTO HEARTS MADE FROM RECYCLED CARD. FAUX CHIC! REAL PINE CONES ARE USED FOR THE PLACE HOLDERS TO GUIDE YOUR GUESTS TO THEIR SEATS.

WOODLAND
WEDDING

Anna

HOW TO MAKE... TABLE CENTREPIECE

MATERIALS

THICK CARDBOARD

TWO LOGS (ONE LARGE, ONE SMALLER)
FOR EACH GUEST TABLE

PINE CONES, ONE FOR EACH GUEST

HESSIAN TWINE

GOOD-QUALITY WRITING PAPER

COLD COFFEE AND SOFT PAINTBRUSH

CUTTING MAT, CRAFT KNIFE AND SCISSORS

PENCIL AND MARKER PEN

SCREWDRIVER

GAS LIGHTER

TIP
If you want a less rustic look, you could spray paint the pine cones to match your wedding colour scheme.

01 To make the guest table number, cut a heart shape from thick cardboard. While you could use a heart template as a guide to the shape, you will get a more realistic result if you draw the shape freehand. Use a craft knife to cut out your heart shape.

02 Working on the cutting mat to protect your work surface, use the screwdriver to make two holes at the top of the heart. If you don't have a cutting mat, place a piece of blu-tack beneath the heart where you want to pierce the holes.

03 Use a pencil to write the guest table number in the middle of the heart. Use the craft knife to go over the number a couple of times, just enough to remove the top surface of the cardboard, to make an incision to give the impression that the number has been carved out.

04 Paint the cardboard heart with several coats of strong, cold coffee to colour it brown (at least three or four). This will make your cardboard heart look more like a piece of wood. To avoid over-wetting the cardboard, be sure to allow a few minutes between coat applications. Leave to dry thoroughly.

05 Once the cardboard heart has dried completely, use the gas lighter to carefully singe its edges to give the impression of the tree bark. For safety's sake, it is a good idea to use a pair of fireproof gloves and to have a bowl of water to hand. Move the flame quickly over the front surface of the heart to distress the carved number further if you wish.

06 Cut a length of twine long enough to wrap around the smaller log and thread it through the holes pierced in the heart. Tie the heart in place.

07 Follow steps 1–6 to make a larger heart decorated with the bride and groom's initials, and tie this around the larger log.

08 Assemble the table centrepiece. Put the small log on top of the large log, positioning it slightly to one side. Place a few pine cones alongside the small log to finish.

09 To make the pine cone place cards, cut rectangles of paper measuring approx 6 x 4cm (2⅜ x1½in) and write on the names of your guests. Now simply insert the tags in the pine cones, making sure that the names can be clearly seen.

SEE P91 & P93 FOR HEART TEMPLATES

ILARIA CHIARATTI

Italian-born Ilaria lives in the Netherlands with her husband. She works as a freelance photographer for the Italian magazine *Casa Facile* and her work has been published in France, China and Russia. She also runs her own company, IDA Interior LifeStyle, an interior design consultancy. She shares her interior styling inspirations and her crochet work on her blog at www.idainteriorlifestyle.com

WEDDING DAY DREAMS

SWEET CAKE TOPPERS

01

A cheese wedding cake is a tasty alternative to the traditional iced cake, and these adorable mice, with their heart-entwined tails, make the perfect decoration to sit on the very top layer. They are made from polymer clay by Melina and Marina Nazarians, twin sisters from southern California. To view more of their handmade collection, visit www.melimaristudio.etsy.com

02

Based in Ljubljana, the capital city of Slovenia, Mojca of CherryTime makes all sorts of lovely things from crochet, including unique and personalised cake toppers. From koi to clown fish, or fish in any colour of the rainbow, she prides herself on being able to customise each happy pair.
www.cherrytime.etsy.com

03

Melanie Ann Green's needle felted snowy owls make the perfect cake topper for a winter wedding. They are made from natural white merino wool with sweet little silver wire legs. To see more of her amazing designs, visit Melanie's felt menagerie at www.feltmeupdesigns.co.uk

SPECIAL TOUCHES

04

Paper Polaroid is a husband-and-wife team making a crafty living in Lancaster County, Pennsylvania. Their decorative paper creations include these romantic paper hearts on sticks, which make wonderfully colourful wedding favours. www.PaperPolaroid.etsy.com

05

Meg, the collage artist behind Vintage Scraps, creates journals, art and cards using forgotten bits of antique papers. These journals feature original, vintage wedding dress pattern illustrations, antique buttons and lace, and they make great retro-look wedding guest books. For more of Meg's designs visit www.VintageScraps.etsy.com

06

These robin's nest place cards are a whimsical way to decorate guest tables at the reception, to guide family and friends to take their places. They were designed by Donni of Fairyfolk Weddings, who is brimming with ideas for natural woodland weddings at www.FairyfolkWeddings.etsy.com

MACHINE APPLIQUÉ
PHOTO ALBUM COVER

PHOTOGRAPHS CAPTURE MEMORIES OF THE DAY THAT THE NEW COUPLE CAN CHERISH FOREVER. A HANDMADE CUSTOMISED ALBUM COVER, DECORATED IN THE STYLE AND COLOURS OF YOUR WEDDING, BRINGS BACK THE EMOTIONS OF THE DAY AT FIRST GLANCE, WITHOUT YOU EVEN HAVING TO TAKE A PEEK INSIDE!

MEMORIES
TO SHARE

elsa ♡ thomas
5.4.2015

HOW TO MAKE... PHOTO ALBUM COVER

SEE P92 FOR TEMPLATES

MATERIALS

PHOTOGRAPH ALBUM 24CM (9¹/₂IN) HIGH BY 21.5CM (8¹/₂IN) WIDE BY 1.8CM (³/₄IN) DEEP

COTTON/LINEN BLEND FABRIC: TWO PIECES FOR THE FRONT AND BACK COVER EACH MEASURING 26 x 20.5CM (10¹/₄ x 8¹/₄IN) AND TWO PIECES FOR THE INSIDE PANELS EACH MEASURING 26 x 12.5CM (10¹/₄ x 5IN)

ONE PIECE OF FLORAL FABRIC FOR THE SPINE MEASURING 26 x 10CM (10¹/₄ x 4IN)

ONE PIECE OF FLORAL FABRIC FOR THE LINING MEASURING 26 x 47CM (10¹/₄ x 18¹/₂IN)

SCRAPS OF FLORAL FABRIC FOR THE APPLIQUÉ

DOUBLE-SIDED FUSIBLE WEBBING

RIBBON AND EMBROIDERY THREADS IN COLOURS TO MATCH THE FLORAL FABRICS

GOOD-QUALITY BLACK SEWING THREAD

EMBROIDERY HOOP AND DARNING/ EMBROIDERY MACHINE PRESSER FOOT

SEWING MACHINE, PENCIL, IRON, SCISSORS, PINS AND NEEDLE

01 Pin the floral fabric spine on top of the cotton/linen front piece with right sides facing, lining up along the left edge. Machine stitch using a 1cm (³/₈in) seam allowance. Press the seams open.

02 Trace the birds, ribbon banner and heart templates onto pieces of double-sided fusible webbing. Use an iron to press the motifs onto the back of your chosen fabric scraps, then cut out carefully around the marked outlines.

03 Peel off the paper backing from the fusible webbing, position the motifs on the album cover front and iron in place. Hoop up the fabric and attach the darning/embroidery foot to your sewing machine.

04 Drop the machine's feed dogs and, using the black thread, freehand

TIP
To calculate the fabric measurements to suit a different sized photo album, measure the width of your album, double it, add the depth of the spine, then add a 1cm (³/₈in) seam allowance all around the edge.

machine embroider around the shapes twice. Add the shading on the ribbon banner, the eyes to the birds and the trailing ribbon to the hanging heart. Trim and neaten the threads at the front and back. Remove the hoop.

05 Now work the hand embroidery. Use a pencil to lightly mark the first names and wedding date onto the ribbon banner. Use a light box (or hold the fabric up against a window) to trace the flower embroidery pattern and corner motifs onto the fabric.

06 Use backstitch to embroider the names/date, and follow the stitch advice on the embroidery patterns for working the flower embroidery and the corner motifs in thread colours to match your fabrics. Complete the running stitch border around the edge of the cover.

07 With right sides facing, pin the cotton/linen back piece to the raw edge of the spine and machine stitch together with a 1cm (³/₈in) seam allowance. Press the seams open. Hem one long edge on each of the cotton/linen fabric inside panels. With the right side of the album

cover facing up, pin the inside panels in place, aligning the raw edges and sandwiching a piece of ribbon centrally at each side (for the ties). Machine stitch around the raw edges with a 6mm (¼in) seam allowance.

08 Pin the lining fabric on top with right sides facing, and machine stitch around the edge of the cover using a 1cm (⅜in) seam allowance, leaving a 3cm (1⅛in) gap at the base of the spine for turning through. Snip the corners and turn the finished cover the right way out. Press and slip stitch the opening closed by hand.

EMILY CARLILL

Emily Carlill crafted her own DIY wedding in 2011. She continues to make lots more wedding crafts for others as well as running her crafty business Love Me Sew, designing and creating craft packs and holding sewing workshops. For more see www.emilycarlill.com and www.lovemesew.co.uk

STITCHED FELT

GOOD LUCK CHARMS

IT IS A TRADITION TO GIVE THE BRIDE A TOKEN TO HOLD ON HER WEDDING DAY, TO WISH HER WELL AND TO BESTOW HER WITH GOOD LUCK. DIFFERENT CULTURES HAVE DIFFERENT GOOD LUCK SYMBOLS — FOR EXAMPLE, IN CHINA, A TURTLE REPRESENTS WEALTH, LONGEVITY AND GOOD HEALTH — AND THERE ARE THREE MORE DESIGNS FOR YOU TO CHOOSE FROM.

TRADITIONAL
FUN

HOW TO MAKE... GOOD LUCK CHARMS

MATERIALS

FELT: DARK GREY, LIGHT GREY, BABY PINK, CANDY PINK, WHITE AND PISTACHIO GREEN

EMBROIDERY OR SEWING THREADS IN SHADES TO MATCH FELT COLOURS

SMALL AMOUNT OF POLYESTER STUFFING

1CM- (⅜IN-) WIDE SATIN RIBBON IN SHADES TO MATCH YOUR FELT COLOURS

PINS, SHARP NEEDLE AND SMALL, SHARP SCISSORS

TIP
Use a medium-density felt – you can change the colours of the charms to match your wedding colour scheme. If you don't have any polyester stuffing, cotton wool will work just as well.

01 Start by cutting out two identical backing shapes for the base of each of the charms using the templates provided. The backing shape is the outer outline on each of the templates, and these should be cut from a contrasting felt colour so that the appliqué really stands out: candy pink has been used for the cat, dark grey for the turtle and white for the cake and horseshoe.

02 Using the templates provided and the finished project photograph on p65 to guide you, cut out all the other pieces of felt that you will need to complete each charm appliqué. Use small sharp scissors to cut the intricate pieces as neatly as possible.

03 Now begin layering and stitching the small details onto the front pieces, such as the ears, eyes and nose onto the cat's head, and the belly and heart onto the cat's body. Use thread to match the felt piece being sewn on, working small back stitches with a sharp embroidery needle. Sew on very small pieces, like the cat's pupils, with tiny cross stitches.

04 Once the front appliqué is layered and stitched, pin the pieces onto one of the backing shapes.

05 Start stitching around the edge of the appliquéd pieces to secure them in place, working your back stitches approx 2mm (³⁄₃₂in) from the edge to mirror the outline of the design. Add any additional stitched details such as the small stitch beneath the cat's nose for the mouth and the progressively longer stitches at either side of the nose for the whiskers.

06 Once all the stitching on the front piece is complete, pin it to the remaining backing piece, taking care to line up front and back as neatly as possible. Blanket stitch around the edge of the charm, leaving a gap for stuffing at the top of the design. Gently fill the charm with stuffing (or cotton wool) but do not overstuff it, as the stuffing may become visible through the blanket stitch edge.

07 Make a small hanging loop from a short length of ribbon, slip it into the stuffing gap and stitch the opening closed. For the horseshoe charm, both of the top edges are left open for stuffing, and a longer length of ribbon is inserted into each opening to make a handle for carrying.

SEE P93
FOR
TEMPLATES

01

02

03

04

CHARLIE MOORBY
aka THE SAVVY CRAFTER

Charlie is a thrifty craft blogger and incurable stitching addict with a penchant for anything handmade. Commissioning Editor by day and crafter by night, you'll find her collecting buttons and hoarding ribbons on a daily basis.
She's a dab hand with a pencil and loves a spot of cross stitching too.
Find her online at
www.thesavvycrafter.com

05

06

07

TIP
The turtle, the horseshoe and the wedding cake charms are made in exactly the same way as the cat. The addition of extra lengths of ribbon on some of the charms adds an extra celebratory touch.

LACE EMBOSSED
WEDDING FAVOURS

MANY COUPLES ENJOY GIVING WEDDING GUESTS A LITTLE GIFT. THESE PRETTY LITTLE BAGS ARE SIMPLE TO MAKE FROM BROWN PAPER AND CAN BE FILLED WITH ANY SWEET TREAT. SEAL EACH WITH A TAG EMBOSSED WITH THE NAMES OF THE HAPPY COUPLE AND TIE IN PLACE WITH SOME PRETTY VINTAGE LACE LAID OVER A MINIATURE DOILY.

FILL WITH
SWEET TREATS

HOW TO MAKE... WEDDING FAVOURS

SEE P93 FOR TEMPLATES

MATERIALS

WHITE AIR-DRY MODELLING CLAY

THICK BROWN PAPER

LACE RIBBON

MINIATURE DOILIES

PATTERNED RUBBER STAMP AND MINIATURE ALPHABET STAMPS

SWEET TREATS

TRACING PAPER, THIN CARD AND PENCILS (HB AND 2H)

ROLLING PIN AND NAIL FILE

CUTTING MAT, CRAFT KNIFE AND METAL RULER

MASKING TAPE AND GLUE STICK

SINGLE HOLE PUNCH AND PAINTBRUSH

TIP
You can choose a patterned paper and any style of ribbon to fit in with the colour scheme of your wedding.

01 Roll out some modelling clay to approx 3mm (⅛in) thick. Trace off the heart template onto thin card, cut it out and use as a template to cut out the heart tags from the clay. For the oblong tags, use the width of a metal ruler to cut strips, then cut the strips into 9cm (3½in) sections.

02 Use a pretty patterned rubber stamp to emboss the bottom of the tags, and the handle of a paintbrush to make a hole approx 1cm (⅜in) down from the top of the tags. Use miniature alphabet stamps to press out the names (or just the initials) of the bride and groom onto the tags. Allow the tags to dry, then use a nail file to smooth off any rough edges.

03 Use a soft HB pencil to trace off the bag template. Turn the tracing paper over, secure the corners to the reverse side of the brown paper with masking tape and go over the marked lines with a hard 2H pencil to give you a nice, sharp outline.

04 Working on a cutting mat, use a metal ruler and a craft knife to cut out the outer edge of the bag shape. Score along all the inner lines and fold them inwards to start forming the bag shape.

05 Run the glue stick along the length of the side strip, overlap this onto the front panel of the bag and press down firmly. Fold in one of the long bottom flaps and run the glue stick along the inside of the other three flaps. Fold in the two small side flaps, then fold the second long flap over the top. Put your fingers inside the bag and press the base against a flat surface, so that the base is securely fixed in place.

06 Squeeze the front and back panels together at the top of the bag to form a crease down the centre of the side panels extending by approx 10cm (4in).

07 Fill the bag with your treats, then take a miniature doily and fold it over the top of the bag to make a closure. Use the single hole punch to make a hole centrally, approx 2.5cm (1in) from the top edge of the bag. Take a 30cm (12in) length of ribbon, thread on one of the tags, then thread the ribbon end through the punched hole. Tie the ribbon in a bow along the top edge of the bag.

DESIGNED
BY CLARE
YOUNGS

PAPER DECORATION

3D DIAMOND GARLAND

PRETTY PAPER 3D DIAMONDS – CORRECTLY KNOWN AS OCTAHEDRA – CAN BE HUNG
SINGLY AROUND YOUR WEDDING VENUE OR STRUNG TOGETHER TO MAKE BEAUTIFUL
GARLANDS. MADE IN THREE DIFFERENT SIZES, EACH IS CUT AND FOLDED FROM
WATERCOLOUR PAPER, PAINTED, EMBELLISHED AND FINISHED WITH A TASSEL.

INSPIRED BY ORIENTAL LANTERNS

HOW TO MAKE... 3D DIAMOND GARLAND

MATERIALS

WATERCOLOUR PAPER (300GSM/140LB)

WATERCOLOUR PAINTS

GOLD LEAF

PATTERNED PAPER

EMBROIDERY THREADS AND YARN

CORD OR STRING

MASKING TAPE OR WASHI TAPE

TRACING PAPER AND PENCIL

CRAFT KNIFE AND METAL RULER

SCISSORS AND PAINTBRUSH

NARROW DOUBLE-SIDED ADHESIVE TAPE

SPRAY ADHESIVE AND GLUE STICK

01 Transfer the 3D diamond garland template onto the watercolour paper and cut it out. Score firmly along the dotted lines, then fold.

02 Brush one or two coats of watercolour paint onto the front of your cut out paper shape (the side without the marked lines) and leave to dry thoroughly.

03 To add gold leaf, mask off one of the triangles by edging it with masking tape or preferably washi tape, as this peels off more easily and is less likely to damage the surface of the paper. Covering the rest of the shape with scrap paper, spray adhesive onto the masked-off triangle. Peel off the tape and press gold leaf on top of the triangle, brushing away any excess at the edges.

TIP
Always make sure you use spray adhesive in a well-ventilated area, and preferably outdoors.

04 To add patterned paper, cut out a triangle from your chosen paper and run a glue stick over the back of it. Position the paper triangle right side up over one of the triangular sections on the watercolour-paper shape and press down carefully.

05 Cut a length of thread measuring 80cm (32in) and fold it in half. Place it in the middle of the paper shape. Add strips of double-sided tape to the flaps, then fold the shape up into a 3D diamond by sticking each flap underneath the edge labelled with the corresponding letter – flap A under side A, flap B under side B and so on. Make sure the folded thread goes through the centre of the diamond as you fold.

06 Cut 15–20 pieces of yarn and thread, each measuring approx 25cm (10in) long. Bundle the threads together and lay them over the loose threads at the bottom of the 3D diamond, using the loose thread to tie a double knot around the centre of the bundle.

TIP
This project requires a card-weight watercolour paper that is fairly substantial but still easy to fold. Hot-pressed is smoother and flatter, so good to embellish with.

DESIGNED BY KIRSTY NEALE

07 Bring all of the thread ends together, then cut an extra piece of thread and tie it around the top of the bundle to form the tassel. Trim the ends for a neat finish.

08 Repeat steps 1–7 to make more 3D diamonds, varying the sizes and colours. Cut a length of cord or string as long as you want your finished garland to be. Slide it through the loop at the top of each 3D diamond in turn, making a single knot to hold each in place.

SEE P92 FOR TEMPLATE

PAINTED GLASS
FLOWER DISPLAY

UPCYCLE A SELECTION OF GLASS JARS AND BOTTLES INTO A STUNNING CENTREPIECE TO GRACE THE TABLES AT YOUR WEDDING RECEPTION BY STENCILLING ON PATTERNS USING METALLIC PAINTS. USE THE DECORATED GLASSWARE AS VASES FOR FRESHLY PICKED FLOWERS OR FILL WITH SMALL BRANCHES DECORATED WITH PRETTY HANDMADE PAPER FLOWER DECORATIONS.

RECYCLED
GLASSWARE

HOW TO MAKE... FLOWER DISPLAY

MATERIALS

GLASS JARS AND BOTTLES

COPPER SPRAY PAINT

WHITE SPIRIT

PAPER DOILIES, ADHESIVE TAPE
IN VARYING WIDTHS, DOT STICKERS
AND TWINE

PATTERNED PAPER

HEART DECORATIONS

TWIGS AND SMALL BRANCHES

SCISSORS, STAPLER AND GLUE

TIP

For the most pleasing results, use both matt and shiny copper spray paint. To make the composition of your centrepiece more interesting, choose different shapes and sizes when selecting jars and bottles.

01 Carefully clean your glass jars and bottles with white spirit and allow to dry thoroughly.

02 Prepare the jars and bottles for painting. Use paper doilies, adhesive tape in varying widths, dot stickers and twine to create a range of different stencil effects when applying your copper spray paint.

03 When applying the copper spray paint, it is safest to work outdoors; if this is not possible, do make sure that doors and windows are left open for a well-ventilated work space. Place the jars in shallow boxes, or protect your work surface with newspaper. Shake the can well and spray 20–30cm (8–12in) away from the jars and bottles. Allow the paint to dry for 6–8 hours.

04 Once the jars and bottles are completely dry, peel off the stencils carefully to reveal the glass beneath.

05 If you prefer a perfect look, clean off any imperfections with a cotton bud dipped into a little white spirit. However, a few wayward paint drips can add a certain charm.

DESIGNED BY ILARIA CHIARATTI

06 To make the paper flowers, cut eight rectangles from your patterned paper each measuring 10 x 35cm (4 x14in). Concertina-fold the rectangles so that the folds measure 1cm (⅜in).

07 Staple in the middle of each of the concertina-folded paper rectangles. Gently open the ends at either side, and staple the ends together to complete each of the paper flowers.

08 Use glue to apply a heart decoration in the centre of the flowers. To make a hanging loop, tie a small piece of twine around one of the stapled ends.

09 Place the painted jars and bottles in the centre of the table, fill with small branches and twigs, and hang up the paper flowers.

NEEDLE FELT
CAKE TOPPER

THIS ADORABLE PAIR OF PLUMP POLAR BEARS MAKES THE CUTEST DECORATION FOR THE TOP OF YOUR WEDDING CAKE. THEY CAN BE CUSTOMISED WITH YOUR OWN SPECIAL TOUCHES. YOU COULD, FOR EXAMPLE, MAKE A TOP HAT FOR THE GROOM, OR A TIARA AND VEIL FOR THE BRIDE, OR PLACE FLOWER- OR HEART-SHAPED BUTTONS BETWEEN THE PAWS.

DARLING DUO

HOW TO MAKE... CAKE TOPPER

MATERIALS

50G OF WHITE OR CREAM MERINO ROVING FOR EACH POLAR BEAR

SMALL AMOUNT OF BLACK MERINO ROVING FOR GROOM'S BOW TIE

FOUR 3mm (1/8IN) GLASS BLACK EYES

BLACK EMBROIDERY THREAD

35–40 SMALL PEARL SEED BEADS

TWO SIZE 40 OR 42 TRIANGULAR FELTING NEEDLES AND HOLDER

ONE SIZE 43 TRIANGULAR FELTING NEEDLE FOR SURFACE FINISHING (OPTIONAL)

FELTING MAT (SPONGE OR BRUSH)

SEWING NEEDLE AND THREAD

TIP

Each bear measures 7–8cm (2¾–3⅛in) with a base width of approx 6cm (2⅜in). You can make larger bears by increasing the amounts of wool roving used, but remember to keep the amounts in proportion.

01 For the main body of the bear, take a 40cm (16in) length of white or cream roving teased out to a strip about 4cm (1½in) wide and fold it over to make a bundle approx 10 x 4cm (4 x 1½in) wide. Take another length of roving approx 30 x 4cm (12 x 1½in), fluff it into a loose ball and insert it into one side of the bundle.

02 Pull the outer edges round to enclose the filling and begin working with two needles to form a fat-bottomed bulb with a tapering point. Keep the filling at one end for a base that is wide and flat beneath.

03 As the wool mats together, start pushing one side inwards to make a fat, curved teardrop shape. When the body feels quite firm, shape the head, holding the wool in place so that the nose points skywards. Use one needle for precision. You now have your basic bear shape.

04 Take a small amount of roving and, working with one needle, make a stumpy tail on the bear's bottom no more than 1cm (⅜in) long.

05 Take very small wisps of wool and loosely shape two tiny ears on the felting mat before needling them onto the front of the head.

06 Make the back legs from a length of roving measuring approx 15 x 4cm (6 x 1½in) split into two equal parts, shaping each part into a leg by doubling the wool over. When the legs are still soft but nicely

shaped, attach them to the bottom of the bear in a sitting position. Make the front legs in the same way, but this time use a length of roving approx10 x 4cm (4 x 1½in), and fix the front legs in between the back legs, pointing them slightly inwards. Each leg should be about 5–6cm (2–2⅜in) when finished, and the thicker tops of the front legs should form the shoulders.

07 Cover the entire body in very thin layers of wool laid in the same direction. Work with one needle (size 43 preferably) for a fine, smooth finish. Sew on the eyes and satin stitch a triangle with black embroidery thread for the nose.

08 To finish the groom, use one felting needle to carefully make a tiny bow tie from a very small wisp of black roving and needle it in place under the bear's chin.

09 Repeat steps 1–7 to make a slightly smaller bear for the bride. Thread the seed beads onto good-quality sewing thread and tie in place around the bride's neck.

GRETEL PARKER

Children's illustrator Gretel Parker discovered needle felting five years ago. Now her work is collected all over the world and she enjoys passing on her knowledge and spreading the needle felting 'bug' to new crafters. www.gretelparker.com

CROCHET LACE
BRIDESMAID'S POSY

MAKE THESE FLOWER-BUD HAIR ACCESSORIES, WHICH ARE ABOUT 4CM (1½IN) IN DIAMETER, TO MATCH YOUR MAIN COLOUR THEME FOR THE BIG DAY. THE DOILY-INSPIRED POSY WRAP, WHICH IS ABOUT 9.5CM (3¾IN) IN DIAMETER, IS WORKED IN ROWS RATHER THAN ROUNDS, GIVING IT AN OPEN SIDE THAT ALLOWS YOU TO WRAP IT AROUND A BOUQUET.

FLORAL
FANCIES

HOW TO MAKE... FLOWER HAIR ACCESSORY & POSY

MATERIALS

ONE 50G BALL (115M/126YD) OF ROWAN COTTON GLACE IN BUBBLES 724 (A), OR SIMILAR YARN (4-PLY COTTON)

ONE 100G BALL (210M/230YD) OF PATONS 100% COTTON DK IN BRIGHT PINK 2725 (B), OR SIMILAR YARN (DK-WEIGHT COTTON)

ONE 50G BALL (208M/227YD) OF ANCHOR ARTISTE BABY SOFT IN CREAM 926 (C), OR SIMILAR YARN (CROCHET COTTON)

SIZE 2MM (US B1) AND SIZE 2.5MM (US C2) CROCHET HOOKS

ONE HAIR CLIP FOR EACH FLOWER-BUD ACCESSORY

ONE SHELL BUTTON AND 100CM (40IN) LENGTH OF 1.5CM- (⅝IN-) WIDE SATIN RIBBON FOR THE POSY WRAP

GLASS-HEADED PINS AND SAFETY PIN

TAPESTRY NEEDLE

01 Crochet the flower hair accessory. Using yarn A and 2.5mm hook, make 29ch plus 1 tch.

Row 1: 1dc into second ch from hook, 1dc into next ch, *work (1dc, 4ch, 1dc) into next ch, 1dc into next 3ch, rep from * five more times, work (1dc, 4ch, 1dc) into next ch, 1dc into last 2ch, turn.

Row 2: 1ch, miss 3 sts, 7tr into first 4ch loop, miss 2 sts, ss into next st, work [7tr into next 4ch loop, miss 2 sts, ss into next st] twice, *miss 2 sts, 7htr into next 4ch loop, miss 2 sts, 1dc into next st, rep from * to end, turn.

Fasten off yarn A and join yarn B.

TIP
Experiment with scale by using a smaller hook and finer yarn or a larger hook and thicker yarn.

Row 1

Row 2

Flower hair accessory chart

● ss   ○ ch   + dc   T htr   ‡ tr

Row 3: 1ch, ss into first st, *1dc into next 2 sts, 2htr into next 3 sts, 1dc into next 2 sts, ss into next st, rep from * three more times.
Fasten off yarn, leaving a long enough length to sew the base of the flower.

02 To shape the flowers, sew in all the loose ends except the length left for sewing up. Starting from the smaller single-colour petals, roll the flower up, making sure that the chain from the beginning of the pattern almost coils around itself like a spiral. Secure the rolled up flower with a pin. Thread a tapestry needle with the remaining length of yarn ready to finish off the flower securely.

03 Secure the base of the rolled up flower by inserting the needle through all the layers. Repeat this several times, working around the base. Sew in the remaining yarn tail. Stitch the flower to the hair clip.

TIP
This flower-bud design will work perfectly no matter what style of clip, clasp, comb or grip you choose to use.

TIP
To add some complementary foliage, cut out a simple felt fabric leaf shape and stitch it to the back of the flower.

Abbreviations

(UK terms used throughout)
ch: chain
dc: double crochet
htr: half treble
MP: make picot
rep: repeat
sp: space
ss: slip stitch
st(s): stitch(es)
tch: turning chain
tog: together
tr: treble
tr2tog: treble two stitches together (decrease by one stitch)
UK/US differences:
UK dc (double crochet) = US sc (single crochet)
UK htr (half treble) = US hdc (half double crochet)
UK tr (treble) = US dc (double crochet)

HOW TO MAKE... POSY (CONTINUED)

TIP
Add beads to the outer edge picots for an extra touch of sparkle.

04 Crochet the bridesmaid's posy wrap. Using yarn C and 2mm hook, work 15ch for foundation row plus 3ch (counts as 1tr).
Row 1: 1tr into fourth ch from hook, 1tr into each ch to end, turn. (16tr)
Row 2: 4ch (counts as 1tr and 1ch), *1tr into next st, 1ch, rep from * 13 times, 1tr into top of 3ch, turn.
Row 3: 5ch (counts as 1tr and 2ch), *1tr into next st, 2ch, rep from * 13 times, 1tr into top of 3ch, turn.
Row 4: Ss into first st and 2ch-sp, 3ch (counts as 1tr), 2tr into same 2ch-sp, *1ch, miss next st, 3tr into next 2ch-sp, rep from * 13 times, turn.
Row 5: Ss into first st, 3ch (counts as 1tr), *work [1tr, 5ch, 1tr] into next st, tr2tog over next 2 sts missing 1ch in between sts, rep from * 13 times, work [1tr, 5ch, 1tr] into next st, 1tr into 3ch, turn.
Row 6: 1ch, ss into first st, *work [2dc, 1htr, make picot (MP) by working 3ch and ss into top of last st worked, 2tr, MP, 1tr, 1htr, MP, 2dc] into 5ch loop, ss into top of tr2tog from previous row, rep from * 14 times, working ss into top of 3ch for final repetition.
Break yarn and weave in ends.

05 Working on a padded surface, block the crochet out using glass-headed pins, making sure to stretch the fabric to open out the design.

06 Place a damp cloth over the top of your pinned-out crochet piece and gently press using a steam iron, then leave to dry thoroughly.

Posy wrap chart

● ss ○ ch + dc ⊤ htr ⊥ tr ⊻ tr2tog

07 Sew on the shell button to the fourth row on the wrong side (the button will fasten to the inside of the design). Fasten the button to close the wrap.

08 Take the ribbon and fasten a safety pin to one end of it. This will help you to guide the ribbon as you weave it in and out of the gaps. Tie the ribbon ends in a bow to finish.

CAROL MELDRUM

Carol is a textile designer, author and workshop tutor based in Glasgow, Scotland, who enjoys nothing better than playing around with yarn, coming up with new ideas and sharing them with folk at www.beatknit.com and blog.beatknit.com

TEMPLATES

ALL THE SHAPES FOR THE BOOK'S MAKES. ENLARGE ALL TEMPLATES BY 200% BY
PHOTOCOPYING THE PAGES, WITH THE EXCEPTION OF RING PILLOW AND 3D DIAMOND
GARLAND ON P92, WHICH SHOULD BE ENLARGED BY 400%. YOU CAN ALSO FIND THE
FULL-SIZE TEMPLATES READY TO DOWNLOAD FROM WWW.LOVECRAFTS.CO.UK

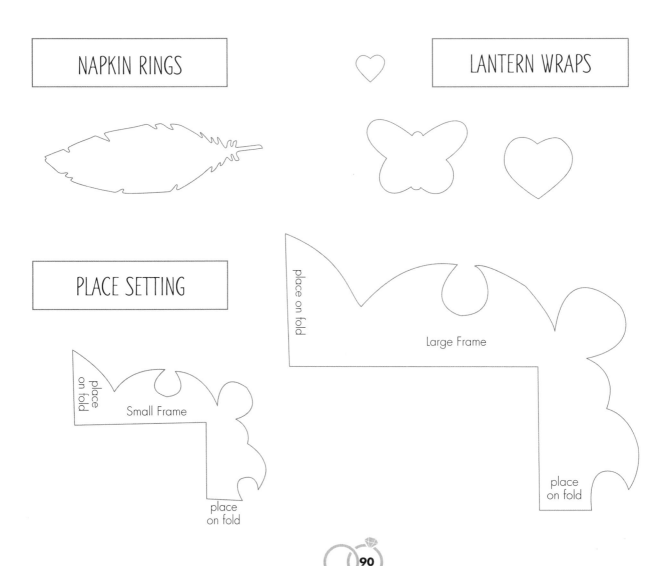

NAPKIN RINGS

LANTERN WRAPS

PLACE SETTING

place on fold

Large Frame

place
on fold

Small Frame

place
on fold

place
on fold

TRUE LOVE CUSHIONS

Heart

Scroll End
cut 2

Scroll

WEDDING DECORATION

Collar

Tie

Waistcoat

CORSAGES & BOUTONNIERES

Large Leaf

cut

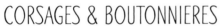

Large Petal

cut

Small Leaf

Small Petal

cut

WEDDING INVITES

leave gap

leave gap

Heart Wreath

leave gap

leave gap

leave gap

Bird

RING PILLOW

A1

1 x satsuma
1 x orange

A2

1 x pale pink

C1

1 x coral

C3

1 x satsuma

C2

1 x peach

A3

1 x bright pink

B1
1 x bright pink

D1

1 x yellow

E1

1 x candy pink
1 x pale pink

B2
1 x peach
1 x coral

D2

1 x bright pink

D3

1 x candy pink

B3

1 x pale pink

E2

1 x orange

E4

1 x coral

E3

1 x yellow

circle

small flower

PHOTO ALBUM COVER

Ribbon Banner

Heart

Bird 2

Bird 1

Corner Motif Embroidery
Pattern

French knot

daisy stitch

running stitch

Flower Embroidery
Pattern

daisy stitch
(DS)

DS

DS

satin stitch

3D DIAMOND GARLAND

Note:
the template
supplied
will make a
15cm (6in)
3D diamond
and it can be
enlarged or
reduced to
make larger
or smaller
sizes.

flap A

flap D

A

D

E

C

flap B

B

flap C

flap E

GOOD LUCK CHARMS

Cake

Turtle

Cat

Horseshoe

Heart

WEDDING FAVOURS

Bag

CHARTS

WEDDING SAMPLER

Cross stitch

Working cross stitch – method 1

Working left to right, make a row of diagonal stitches. Up at 1, down at 2, up at 3. Repeat. Working right to left, complete the Xs with a row of diagonal stitches. Up at 4, down at 5, up at 6. Repeat.

Working cross stitch – method 2

Work left to right. Up at 1, down at 2, up at 3. Down at 4, up at 5. Repeat.

Finishing a thread

Slide the needle through five to six stitches on the back of your work to secure and finish off the thread.

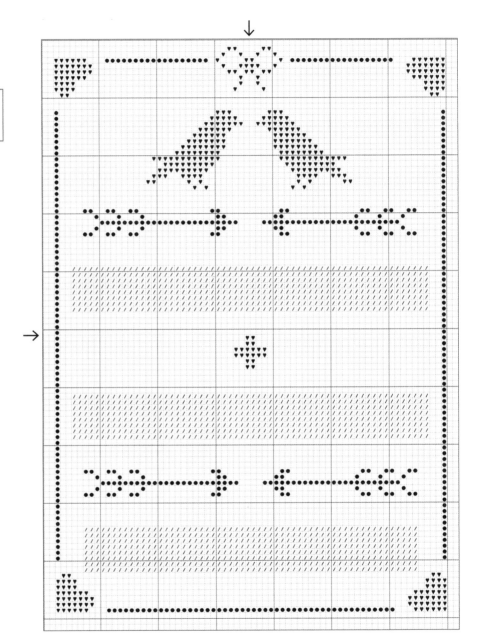

Key

♥ Anchor 926/DMC 712

● Anchor 366/DMC 739

/ Add name/date here

Key

♥ Anchor 926/DMC 712

PUBLISHER'S ACKNOWLEDGEMENTS

This book would not have been possible without the input of all our crafty contributors, who have provided all our brilliant how-to projects and step-by-step photography. We would also like to thank Cheryl Brown, who has done an excellent job of pulling everything together, and Sophie Martin for her design layout. Thanks to Mollie Johanson for allowing us to use her stitch diagrams. Main project photography by Rachel Whiting. And of course, thanks must go to the fantastic team at Mollie Makes for all their help, in particular Lara Watson, Helena Tracey, Jane Toft and Katherine Raderecht.

For more information
on Mollie Makes
please visit
www.molliemakes.com

Whatever the craft, we have the book for you – just head straight to Collins & Brown crafty HeadQuarters!

LoveCrafts is the one-stop destination for all things crafty, with the very latest news and information about all our books and authors. It doesn't stop there…

Enter our fabulous competitions and win great prizes
Download free patterns from our talented authors
Collect LoveCrafts loyalty points and receive special offers on all our books

Join our crafting community at LoveCrafts – we look forward to meeting you!

First published in the United Kingdom in 2014 by
Collins & Brown
10 Southcombe Street
London
W14 0RA

An imprint of Anova Books Company Ltd

ISBN 978-1-90939-730-9

A CIP catalogue record for this book is available from the British Library.

10 9 8 7 6 5 4 3 2 1

Reproduction by Mission, Hong Kong
Printed by 1010 Printing International Ltd, China

This book can be ordered direct from the publisher at
www.anovabooks.com